# Applying the Standards:
# Evidence-Based Writing
## Grade 3

**Credits**
Author: Nancy Rogers Bosse
Copy Editor: Karen Seberg

Visit carsondellosa.com for correlations to Common Core, state, national, and Canadian provincial standards.

Carson-Dellosa Publishing, LLC
PO Box 35665
Greensboro, NC 27425 USA
carsondellosa.com

ISBN 978-1-4838-1455-1
01-005151151

# Table of Contents

# Introduction

Common Core writing standards focus on three main text types: opinion/argumentative, informative/explanatory, and narrative. A fourth category, research writing, is essential to any evidence-based writing program.

Research shows that effective writing strategies include every step of the writing process: prewriting/brainstorming, drafting, revising, editing/proofreading, and publishing. Students will be walked through these steps on pages 6–10. The Writing Practice Packet can be reused for additional practice by changing the topic.

The writing exercises in this book are designed to go beyond basic writing conventions. Students will learn how to base opinions on evidence, infer facts from relevant details, convey accurate background information, and recount real or imagined experiences. Students' critical thinking skills are engaged when they do research, consider and analyze information, and respond to writing prompts. Writing prompts are paired with graphic organizers and followed by thinking/writing challenges.

# Common Core Alignment Chart

Use this chart to plan instruction, practice, or remediation of a standard.

| Common Core State Standards* | | Practice Pages |
|---|---|---|
| **Writing Standards** | | |
| Text Types and Purposes | 3.W.1–3.W.3 | 11–63 |
| Production and Distribution of Writing | 3.W.4–3.W.6 | 11, 12, 14–18, 20, 23, 24, 30, 32, 33, 37–43, 45, 46, 48–50, 56, 57, 59–61 |
| Research to Build and Present Knowledge | 3.W.7–3.W.9 | 11, 12, 15, 18, 19, 21–38, 46–48, 51–63 |
| Range of Writing | 3.W.10 | Adapt writing prompts to cover this standard. |
| **Language Standards** | | |
| Conventions of Standard English | 3.L.1–3.L.2 | 11–13, 15–17, 19, 21, 23–26, 30, 31, 33–38, 40–46, 51, 52–54, 56–63 |
| Knowledge of Language | 3.L.3 | 14, 18, 48, 49 |
| Vocabulary Acquisition and Use | 3.L.4–3.L.6 | 20, 22, 25, 27–29, 32, 39, 47, 50, 55 |

# About This Book

Use this book to teach your students to read closely, or to notice words, structure, and points of fact. The writing prompts that begin on page 11 are intended to engage students' interests and then to send them off on a hunt for more information. Graphic organizers will help students organize their thoughts and research notes. Their actual writing will take place on separate sheets of paper. Encourage students to share their writing with peers, teachers, and other adults. Show students how to use the Student Writing Checklist on page 5. Allow time for thoughtful revisions. Publication is an important Common Core component of writing standards; students should be given access to computers, tablets, or copying machines.

# Common Core-Aligned Writing Rubric

Use this rubric as a guide to assess students' written work. You may also offer it to students to help them check their work or as a tool to show your scoring.

| | |
|---|---|
| **4** | _____ Offers insightful reasoning and strong evidence of critical thinking<br><br>_____ Responds skillfully to all of the items in the prompt<br><br>_____ Uses a logical organizational structure, including introductory and concluding sentences or paragraphs<br><br>_____ Skillfully connects ideas with linking words and phrases<br><br>_____ Uses vivid dialogue where appropriate<br><br>_____ Skillfully supports topic(s) and opinions with evidence |
| **3** | _____ Offers sufficient reasoning and evidence of critical thinking<br><br>_____ Responds to all items in the prompt<br><br>_____ Uses introductory and concluding sentences<br><br>_____ Connects ideas with appropriate linking words and phrases<br><br>_____ Uses dialogue where appropriate<br><br>_____ Supports topic(s) and opinions with evidence |
| **2** | _____ Demonstrates some evidence of critical thinking<br><br>_____ Responds to some items in the prompt<br><br>_____ Shows some understanding of paragraph formation<br><br>_____ Connects some ideas with linking words and phrases<br><br>_____ Uses some dialogue where appropriate<br><br>_____ Supports topic(s) and opinions with little evidence |
| **1** | _____ Demonstrates limited or no evidence of critical thinking<br><br>_____ Responds to some or no items in the prompts<br><br>_____ Shows little or no understanding of paragraph structure<br><br>_____ Presents ideas or events in random sequence<br><br>_____ Uses little or no dialogue where appropriate<br><br>_____ Topic(s) or opinions are not supported by evidence. |

# Student Writing Checklist

## Prewrite/Brainstorm

_____ Consider and choose the topic for your essay.

_____ Research your topic on the Internet, in books, or in magazines.

_____ Take notes.

_____ Summarize what you have learned.

## Draft

_____ Organize the essay by topics. Separate topics by paragraphs.

_____ Provide an introduction, a body, and a conclusion in the essay.

_____ Support opinions and points of view with reasons.

_____ Develop the topic with facts and definitions.

_____ Include details to describe thoughts, feelings, or actions.

_____ Show evidence in your writing (_for example, because, The author said, I noticed on page ____, Based on what I read online_).

## Revise

_____ Write each sentence with a subject and verb.

_____ Sequence events in the order they occurred.

_____ Make sure sentence meaning is clear.

_____ Use specific nouns, lively verbs, and interesting adjectives.

_____ Use a variety of sentence structures.

## Edit/Proofread

_____ Indent each paragraph.

_____ Capitalize the first letter in each sentence.

_____ Capitalize all proper nouns.

_____ Spell all words correctly.

_____ Use proper grammar, including subject/verb agreement.

_____ Use proper punctuation, including quotation marks.

## Publish

_____ Make sure your final copy is neat—no wrinkles, creases, or holes.

_____ Erase any smudges or dirty spots.

_____ Use good spacing between words.

_____ Use your best handwriting or typing.

_____ Include illustration(s) if appropriate.

## Step 1: Prewrite/Brainstorm

Read the prompt. Think about, plan, and organize your writing. Use the Internet, books, or magazines to find new information about your topic. Use the organizer to take notes.

**Prompt:** What is your favorite sports team or music group? Give reasons for your response.

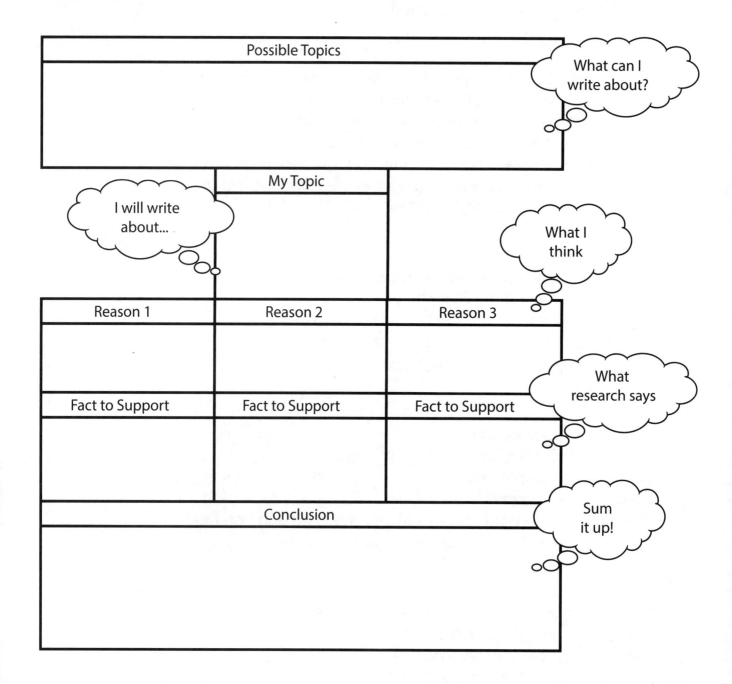

## Step 2: Draft

Use the information from the organizer on page 6. Write a paragraph about your topic. Remember to give reasons to support your opinion. Use linking words or phrases such as *because* and *for example*. In your conclusion, restate your opinion.

_____

_____

_____

_____

_____

_____

_____

_____

_____

_____

_____

_____

_____

_____

_____

_____

_____

_____

_____

_____

_____

## Step 3: Revise

Read your paragraph. Then, answer the questions.

_____ Did I start my paragraph with an interesting introduction that will make readers want to read more?

_____ Did I list reasons to support my opinion?

_____ Did I use words such as *because* and *for example* to link my reasons with my opinion?

_____ Are all of my sentences about the topic?

_____ Should I add more details?

_____ Have I used exciting verbs?

_____ Have I used interesting adjectives?

_____ Have I used the same words too often?

_____ Does my conclusion provide a good summary?

| The best part of this paragraph is | The part that needs a little work is |
|---|---|
| | |

# Step 4: Edit/Proofread

Place a check mark before each item when you have checked your work.

## My Paragraph

_____ I have read my paragraph, and it makes sense.
_____ It has an introduction, body, and conclusion.
_____ I stayed on topic.
_____ My sentences are easy to understand.
_____ I used a variety of words.

## Capitalization

_____ Each sentence begins with a capital letter.
_____ All proper nouns begin with capital letters.
_____ My title words are capitalized except for articles and prepositions.

## Punctuation

_____ Each sentence ends with the correct ending punctuation.
_____ I have placed commas where they belong.
_____ I have used quotation marks to show where speech starts and ends.

## Spelling

_____ I have checked to see that all of the words are spelled correctly.
_____ I have looked up words when needed.

## Grammar

_____ My subjects and verbs match.
_____ I have used suffixes and prefixes properly.
_____ I have used italics or underlining to mark titles of works.

### Peer Editing Checklist

Ask another student or teacher to look at your essay and circle *Yes* or *No*.

| | | |
|---|---|---|
| Does the first word of each sentence start with a capital? | Yes | No |
| Are the proper nouns capitalized? | Yes | No |
| Does each sentence end with a punctuation mark? | Yes | No |
| Are the words spelled correctly? | Yes | No |
| Are the paragraphs indented? | Yes | No |
| Is the handwriting or typing easy to read? | Yes | No |

Editor's Name _____

## Step 5: Publish

When you publish your writing, you make it possible for others to read it. Your readers might be teachers, students, or family members.

1. I choose to publish my writing by

   _____ writing it in neat handwriting.

   _____ typing it on a computer.

   _____ typing it on a tablet.

   _____ copying it on a copier.

2. If I use a cover page, it will include

   _____ the title.

   _____ the author's name.

   _____ the illustrator's name.

   _____ art or decoration.

3. If appropriate, my presentation will include

   _____ illustration(s) or art.

   _____ captions for the illustration(s) or art.

   _____ a graph, chart, or time line.

4. I will share my writing with

   _____   _____

   _____   _____

Name _____

## We All Scream for Ice Cream

Do you like ice cream? Many people enjoy this cool treat. Vanilla is a favorite flavor. But, there are many flavors. What is your favorite?

Search the Internet to find different flavors of ice cream. Ask your friends about their favorites. Choose your favorite flavor. Then, write an advertisement. Convince others to try the flavor. Use your senses. Use descriptive words.

**Prewrite:** Use the organizer to plan your writing.

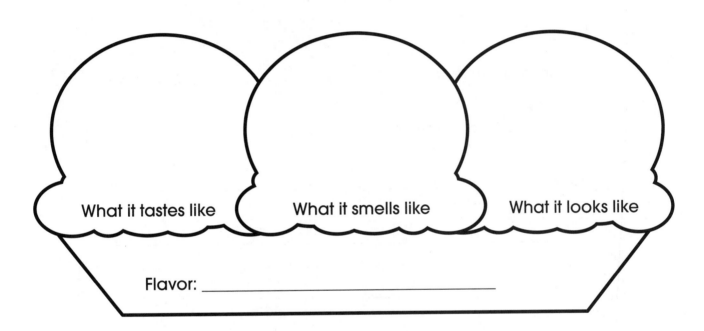

What it tastes like        What it smells like        What it looks like

Flavor: _____

## Reflect and Revise

1. How would you change your advertisement if you wanted to *discourage* someone from trying your favorite flavor of ice cream? Change at least three words in your advertisement.

2. Consider your choice of words and phrases. Revise your writing to be more descriptive.

Name _____

# Problems and Solutions

In a speech, US President John F. Kennedy said, "Ask not what your country can do for you—ask what you can do for your country." Do you agree with President Kennedy? Do you think people should ask what they can do? Or, do you think that the government should solve the problems?

Use the Internet and talk with adults. Find out more about the problems in your country. Talk about who should solve the problems. Write a speech about one problem. State the problem. Then, name who you think should solve the problem. Give three reasons for your opinion.

**Prewrite:** Use the organizer to plan your speech.

Problem in your country: _____

Who should solve the problem: _____

Reason 1: _____

_____

Reason 2: _____

_____

Reason 3: _____

_____

## Reflect and Revise

1. All families have problems. All schools have problems. All groups have problems. So, of course, all countries have problems. Why do you think this is true?

2. Check your speech for capitalization, punctuation, and spelling.

# Reduce, Reuse, Recycle

Can you imagine a ton of garbage? What about 251 million tons (227.7 MT) of garbage? That's the amount of garbage Americans make in a year. Where does garbage go? It is either burned or buried. And, that's not good for the environment. People need to reduce, reuse, and recycle.

What can you do to reduce, reuse, and recycle? Look in books or on the Internet. Write a letter to convince your family to reduce, reuse, and recycle. Include reasons in your letter.

**Prewrite:** Use the organizer to list ways people can cut down on garbage.

| Reduce | Reuse | Recycle |
|--------|-------|---------|
|        |       |         |

## Reflect and Revise

1. Use the information from your organizer to write a television commercial asking people to reduce, reuse, and recycle. Consider making a video of your commercial to show to the class.

2. Reread your letter. Use words such as *also*, *another*, and *more* to connect your ideas.

# Chocolate Chips in the Cookie of Life

Someone said that friends are the chocolate chips in the cookie of life. Friends make everything sweeter. Everyone needs a friend. What do you look for in a friend?

Make a list of qualities you look for in a friend. Talk to others. Add their ideas. Place a star next to the most important quality. Write this quality at the top of the second column. Write three reasons you think this quality is important. Then, write a paragraph. In the first sentence, state the quality. Support your opinion with three reasons.

**Prewrite:** Use the organizer to plan your writing.

| Qualities of a good friend | Most important quality |
|---|---|
| • | |
| • | Reason 1 |
| • | |
| • | Reason 2 |
| • | |
| • | Reason 3 |
| | |

## Reflect and Revise

1. Think about someone you know who has the quality you chose as most important. Then, think of an example of how the person shows this quality. Use this example in your paragraph to support your opinion.

2. Reread your paragraph. Use words such as *because, therefore, since,* and *for example* to connect your ideas.

Name _____

# And the Winner Is . . .

Movie awards are given to the best actor and best actress in a movie. Television also gives awards for the best actor and best actress in a TV show. Books have various awards, including the Pulitzer Prize. But, there are no awards for the best characters in a book. If there were, who do you think should win the best character in a book?

Write a speech telling about your favorite character in a book. Give three reasons. Then, talk to your friends and get their opinions. Ask them for reasons. Use their ideas to make your reasons more powerful.

**Prewrite:** Use the organizer to plan your speech.

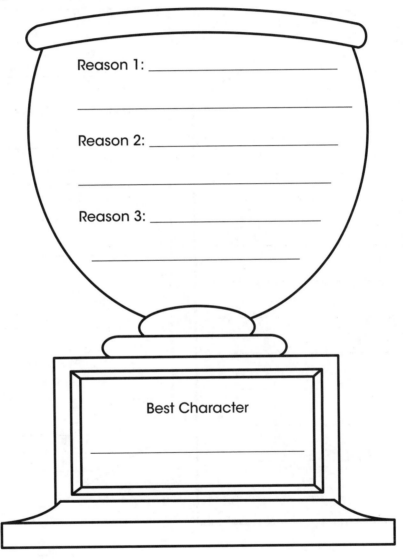

Reason 1: _____

_____

Reason 2: _____

_____

Reason 3: _____

_____

Best Character

_____

 **Reflect and Revise**

1. Do you think such a big deal should be made of awards for television programs and movies? Explain.

2. Reread your speech. Look at the nouns and adjectives you used. Revise your writing. Use interesting adjectives to describe each noun.

Name _____

# To View or Not to View

Do you have a TV? Claire's parents disagree about owning a TV. Claire's dad wants a TV to watch sports. He likes other shows too. Claire's mom thinks TV harms the imagination. She thinks it keeps kids from reading.

Write pros and cons for owning a TV. Use the Internet to find information about watching TV. Then, write an argument for or against owning a TV. State your opinion. Provide at least three reasons. End your argument by restating your opinion.

**Prewrite:** Use the organizer to plan your writing.

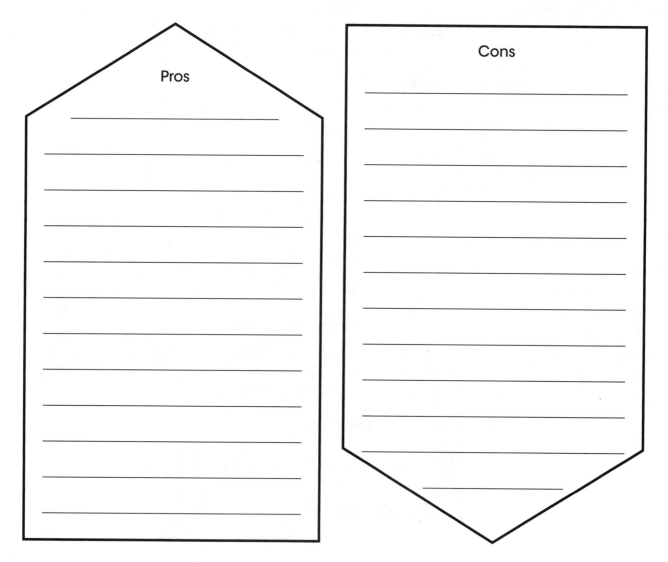

## Reflect and Revise

1. Think of a compromise Claire's parents could make about owning a TV. Write the compromise on another sheet of paper.

2. Reread your argument. Edit your writing. Check for correct capitalization, punctuation, and spelling.

# A Strong Community

Many workers keep a community safe and happy. The police protect. The mail carriers bring mail. The store workers sell things you need. Community workers help in many different ways.

Choose a community worker. Use the Internet or a book to find out about the worker's job. Find three ways this person helps the community. Write a thank-you letter to the worker. Use a computer to write your letter.

**Prewrite:** Use the organizer to list three ways the community worker helps the community.

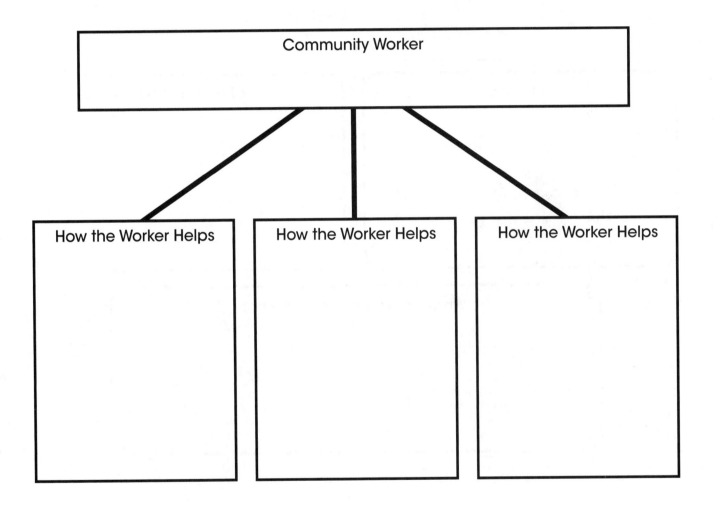

## Reflect and Revise

1. Do you think it is important to thank people for doing their jobs? Why or why not?

2. Consider sending your letter to the community worker. You don't need a name. You can use the worker's job title. Before you send your letter, check your spelling. Use a dictionary if needed.

# Happy Holidays!

Holidays are special days. The word *holiday* comes from the words *holy* and *day*. Many holidays are religious. What is your favorite holiday? What do you know about the holiday? When did the holiday start? Why was the holiday started?

Learn about your favorite holiday. Talk to your family. Look on the Internet. Then, write an essay. Tell why the holiday is your favorite. Support your opinion with facts. Include a picture.

**Prewrite:** Use the organizer to take notes.

## My Favorite Holiday

_____

| What I know | What my family knows |
|---|---|
|  |  |

What I learned on the Internet

 **Reflect and Revise**

1. Did you learn something new about your favorite holiday? If so, write about how the new information changes the way you think about the holiday. If not, do some more research. There is always more to learn.

2. Reread your essay. Revise your sentences to include at least one simple, one compound, and one complex sentence.

Name _____

# Strong Facts

Do you hate the word *no*? The word *no* can be annoying when it is the answer to a request for something you want. Maybe you want a new video game. Maybe you want a later bedtime. But, sometimes the word *no* can be turned into a *yes*. The best way to turn a *no* into a *yes* is to provide strong facts.

Think of something you want that you might not be allowed to do or have. Do research. Find two strong facts that support your request. Then, write a letter stating what you want. Include the two facts. Try to change the person's mind.

**Prewrite:** Use the organizer to take notes.

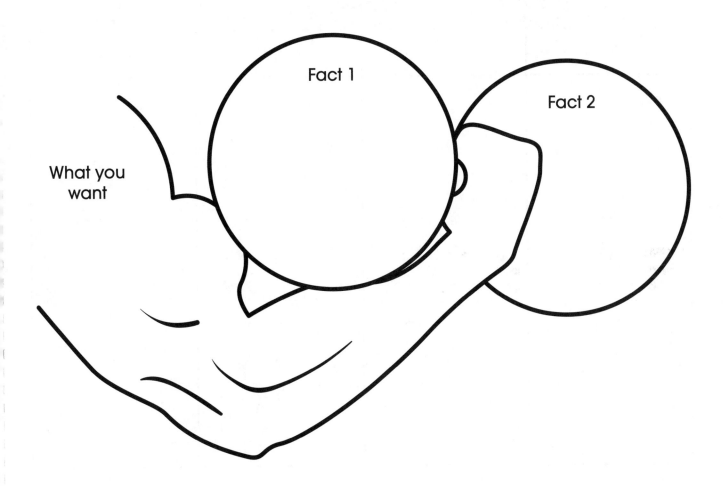

Fact 1

Fact 2

What you want

---

## ✳ Reflect and Revise

1. Write an argument from the point of view of the person saying *no*. Include the facts the person might offer.

2. Reread your letter. Check your spelling. Use a dictionary if needed.

Name _____

# Stay in Touch

Long ago people used the telegraph to stay in touch. Your grandparents used dial phones and letters. Today, people use email and cell phones. What is the best way to stay in touch?

Think of the pros and cons for using cell phones and email. Write your ideas on the organizer. Talk to others about their ideas. Add their ideas to the organizer. Write a paragraph about the best way to stay in touch. State your opinion. Then, support your opinion using the pros and cons. End your paragraph with a concluding sentence.

**Prewrite:** Use the organizer to plan your writing.

| Cell Phone | | Email | |
|---|---|---|---|
| Pros | Cons | Pros | Cons |
| | | | |

## ☀ Reflect and Revise

1. Why is it important to stay in touch? Revise your opening sentence to include why keeping in touch is important. Think of an opening that will catch your readers' attention.

2. Reread your paragraph. Replace at least one word with a synonym. Choose a synonym that adds to the meaning.

 © Carson-Dellosa · CD-104826 · Applying the Standards: Evidence-Based Writing

Name _____

# Let's Move!

First Lady Michelle Obama started Let's Move! This program encourages kids to be active. Being active helps kids stay fit. How do you keep fit?

Maybe you like to play soccer. Or, maybe you like to swim. List three movement activities you enjoy. Then, use the Internet to see how the activities help you stay fit. How many calories do your activities burn? Look for other benefits. Which of your activities is the best? Choose one. Write a pledge to yourself. Start by telling the activity and a goal. Add three sentences telling the benefits of your activity.

**Prewrite:** Use the organizer to plan your writing.

| Activities I Enjoy | Benefits |
|---|---|
|  |  |
|  |  |
|  |  |

## Reflect and Revise

1. Work to keep your pledge. After a week, write about how well you kept your pledge. Revise your pledge if needed.

2. Look at the words you used. Underline words with more than one meaning, such as the word *fit*. Write a definition for each underlined word as it is used in your pledge. Use a dictionary if needed.

# That's Amazing!

The largest omelet was made with 145,000 eggs. Now, that's amazing! Guinness World Records is all about amazing. Since 1955, they have inspired people to do amazing things.

Go to the Guinness World Records website. Look for an amazing feat. Read and take notes. Then, write a news article about the feat. State the evidence you found. Include a picture.

**Prewrite:** Use the organizer to take notes.

| Amazing Feat | |
|---|---|
| The picture showed me . . . | The article said . . . |
| The article said . . . | The article said . . . |

## Reflect and Revise

1. Write about a record you would like to break. Why do you want to break this record?

2. Write a definition for the word *feat*. Then, write three synonyms for the word. Use a thesaurus if needed.

Name _____

# In the Mood

In the book *Judy Moody Was in a Mood* by Megan McDonald (Candlewick Press, 2000), Judy Moody is in a bad mood. What puts you in a bad mood? What helps you get out of a bad mood?

Read the book or talk to your friends. Find out what puts others in bad moods. Find out how they get out of bad moods. Then, write a paragraph telling the best way to get out of a bad mood. Start by stating things that put people in bad moods. Then, list ways to get out of a bad mood. End your paragraph by telling what you think is the best way to get out of a bad mood.

**Prewrite:** Use the organizer to take notes.

| Bad Moods | |
|---|---|
| What puts me in a bad mood | What gets me out of a bad mood |
| What puts others in a bad mood | What gets others out of a bad mood |
| Best way to get out of a bad mood | |

## ☀ Reflect and Revise

1. Write about a time you helped someone get out of a bad mood. What did you do? How did it work?

2. Write a catchy title for your paragraph. Your title should grab the readers' attention. Be sure to capitalize the words in your title correctly.

Name _____

# Superpowers

Superman is super strong. Flash is super fast. Batman has super skills. All superheroes have superpowers. Talk with your friends. Make a list of superpowers.

Choose a superpower you would like to have. Give reasons for your choice. Look on the Internet to learn about the superpower. Use the evidence to support your reasons. Write a paragraph about the superpower. Use words such as *first*, *second*, and *third* to connect your ideas. Be sure to write a conclusion.

**Prewrite:** Use the organizer to plan your writing.

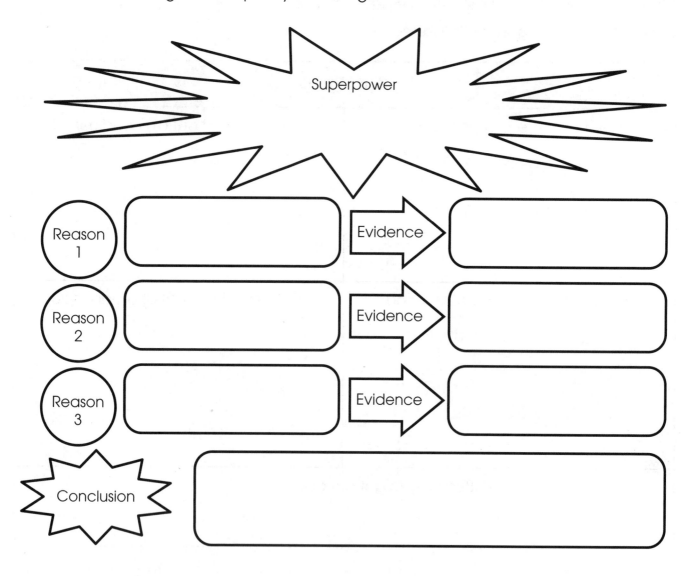

## Reflect and Revise

1. You may not have superpowers, but you have talents. In your conclusion, write about how you can use your talents to do good.

2. Check your writing to see if you used correct verb forms. Revise your verbs as needed.

## Animal Homes

A bee lives in a hive. In fact, a hive can be home to more than 50,000 bees. Beavers build dams and lodges. Birds build nests. Many animals build their own homes.

Choose an animal that builds its own home. Then, do some research. Write a paragraph about the animal and its home. Include a picture.

**Prewrite:** Use the organizer to plan your writing.

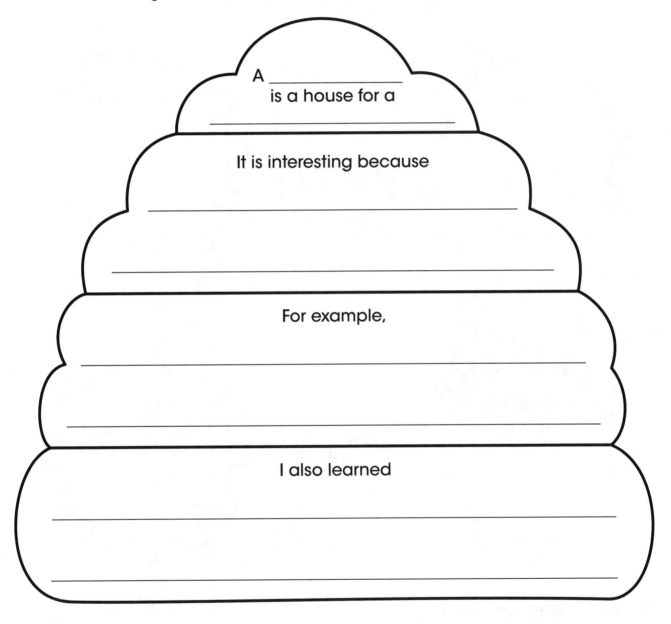

A _____
is a house for a
_____

It is interesting because

_____

_____

For example,

_____

_____

I also learned

_____

_____

## Reflect and Revise

1. What makes your home special? Write about what you love about your house.

2. Revise your paragraph. Underline each noun. Then, include an adjective to describe each noun.

Name _____

# Machines at Work

Look around you. You will probably see a machine that makes life easier. All machines are made up of simple machines. Simple machines include a lever, pulley, inclined plane, wedge, screw, and wheel and axle.

Choose a machine. Use the Internet and books to find out more about the machine. Then, write a short guide about your machine. Include pictures or diagrams.

**Prewrite:** Use the organizer to plan your writing.

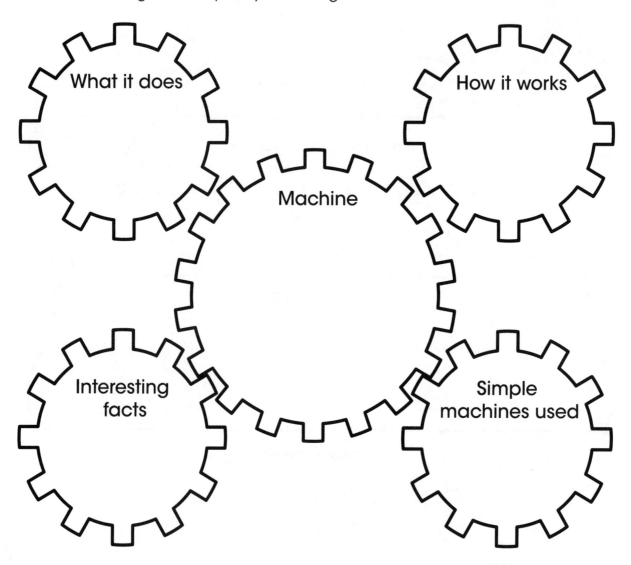

## Reflect and Revise

1. Think about the machine you chose. How would life be different without it? Ask your friends and family for ideas. Add a paragraph to your guide explaining how the machine makes life easier or more fun.

2. Build your vocabulary by including at least four science words in your guide. Create a glossary at the end of the guide.

 © Carson-Dellosa · CD-104826 · Applying the Standards: Evidence-Based Writing

# A Strong Attraction

Magnets are everywhere. Magnets are used in compasses, computers, trains, vending machines, and much more.

What do you know about magnets? What do you want to know? Use the Internet and books to learn more. Create a picture book. Write the book to teach preschoolers about magnets. Create the pages of your book on a computer. Use words and pictures.

**Prewrite:** Use the chart to organize the information. Place a star by at least five facts you want to include in your book.

| Magnets | | |
|---|---|---|
| What I **K**now | What I **W**ant to Know | What I **L**earned |
|  |  |  |

## 🔆 Reflect and Revise

1. Think about what you like about magnets. Then, design a new use for a magnet. Draw a picture and write about it. Include this as the last page in your book.

2. Reread your book. Look at the words you chose. Will preschoolers understand each word? Change at least two words by using synonyms that are easier to understand.

# The Circle of Life

Life is like a circle. Every living thing goes through a cycle. This cycle starts at the beginning of life. Then, each living thing grows. As living things grow, they change. Each living thing becomes an adult. Finally, every living thing dies. This cycle happens with every plant and animal.

Choose a plant or an animal. Look on the Internet or in a book to find information about its life cycle. Then, write a paragraph. Explain the life cycle of your plant or animal. Start your paragraph with a topic sentence. Support the topic sentence with facts and details. Include pictures.

**Prewrite:** Use the graphic organizer to take notes.

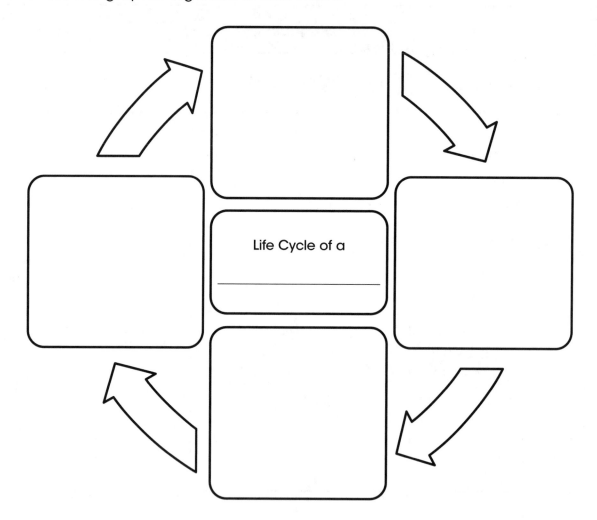

Life Cycle of a
_____

## Reflect and Revise

1. Do you have grandparents? Do you have a baby in your family? Write about your family's circle of life.

2. Look at the notes on your organizer. Circle three words that are new to you or have special meaning when used in science. Define these words in your paragraph.

# Keeping Clean!

Exercise and nutrition are important for good health. But, being clean is another way to stay healthy. Germs can cause illness. Food left on teeth can cause cavities. Keeping clean is important to keeping healthy.

Think about ways you keep yourself clean. Ask an adult for other ways to keep clean. Then, use the Internet or a book to find reasons to keep clean. Write an article for a health book explaining important habits for good health. Write a title for your article. Include pictures.

**Prewrite:** Add the information to the organizer.

| Keeping Clean | |
|---|---|
| What I know | Why it's important |
|  |  |
| What an adult knows | Why it's important |
|  |  |
| What I learned from research | Why it's important |
|  |  |

## ☀ Reflect and Revise

1. Make a list of products people use to keep clean, such as soap and shampoo. Use your imagination to invent a new type of product that would make it easier or more fun to keep clean. Create an ad for your new product.

2. Type your article about healthy habits on a computer. Check for proper spelling and capitalization.

## Itsy Bitsy Spider

Remember this nursery rhyme? *The itsy bitsy spider crawled up the waterspout.* This rhyme makes spiders seem cute. But, some people are afraid of spiders.

Use the Internet or a book to learn more about spiders. Find eight facts. Use the facts to create a book about spiders. Include a picture on each page.

**Prewrite:** Use the organizer to take notes.

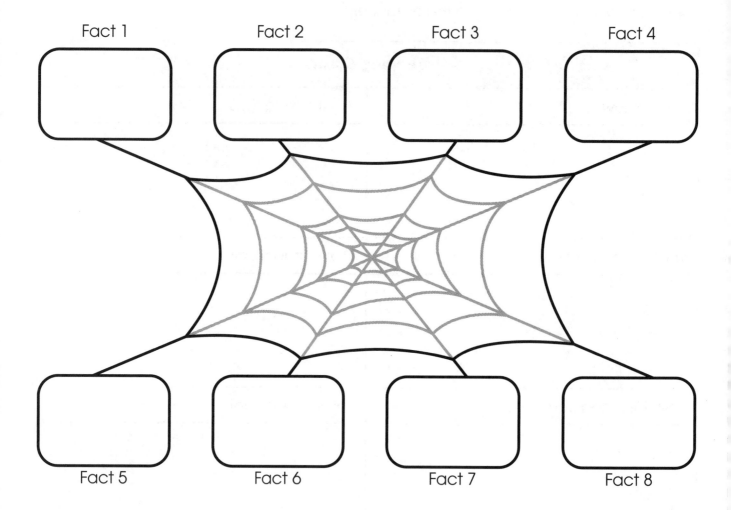

Fact 1   Fact 2   Fact 3   Fact 4

Fact 5   Fact 6   Fact 7   Fact 8

## ✸ Reflect and Revise

1. How do you feel about spiders? Did you change your mind after doing research? Write your opinion about spiders. Give reasons for your opinion. Include your opinion on an introduction page at the beginning of the book.

2. Reread your opinion. Check that your sentences are complete. Revise any fragments or run-ons.

# Where in the World?

There are many amazing places in the world. There are natural parks such as Yosemite. There are fun amusement parks across the country. There are museums such as the Louvre in France. Where would you like to go?

Choose a location. Use the Internet or travel books to do research. Create a travel brochure about the location. Use a brochure format on a computer. Or, create a brochure by folding a sheet of paper into thirds. Ask an adult to help you. Then, create a cover including a title and picture.

**Prewrite:** Use the organizer to group the information.

| Where is _____? | What can you do there? | How do you get there? |
|---|---|---|
| | | |
| | | What are the costs? |
| | | |

## ☀ Reflect and Revise

1. Do you think travel is worth the cost? Explain your answer with reasons.

2. Check your brochure for correct spelling, capitalization, and punctuation.

# In the News

What's happening in your world? Studies show that many kids today don't care about news. Is that true for you? News can be sad and scary, but knowing about current events can be helpful. It is important to know what is happening around the world. There are many news stories that are written for children. These stories are written in a way kids can understand.

Choose a current event. Find a website that is written for kids. Read about the event on the Internet. Then, write a newspaper article about the event. Write your article on a computer.

**Prewrite:** Use the organizer to take notes.

| Headline | |
|---|---|
| Who? | What? |
| When? | |
| Where? | Why? |

## ✺ Reflect and Revise

1. Why do you think many kids are not interested in news? Talk to your friends and get their ideas too. Then, write a paragraph explaining your thoughts.

2. Check your article for correct spelling, capitalization, and punctuation.

Name _____

## What a Character!

Do you know these book characters? Greg Heffley is wimpy. India Opal Buloni is lonely. Nick Allen is clever. We all can relate to some characters in a book. What are you reading now? Who is your favorite character?

Choose a character from a book you are reading. Select one trait that describes the character. Then, look for evidence in the book. Ask a friend or an adult to help you. Write a character sketch describing the trait. Use details from the book.

**Prewrite:** Use the organizer to take notes.

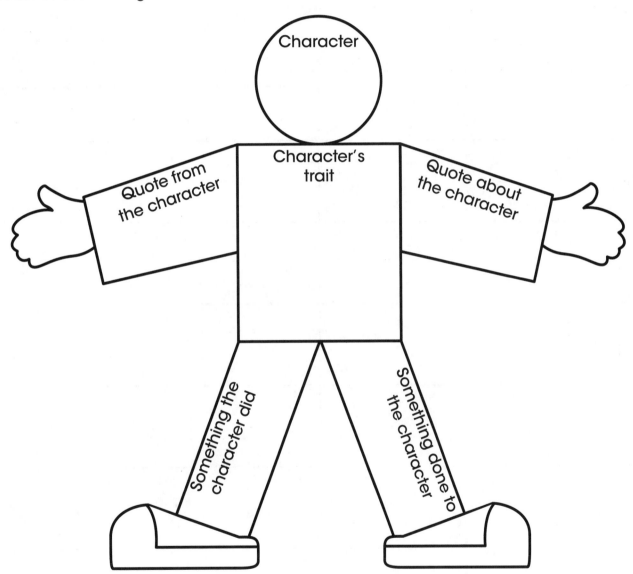

## ☀ Reflect and Revise

1. How are you alike or different from the character you chose? Create a Venn diagram. Add a paragraph comparing yourself to the character.

2. Check your character sketch for correct spelling, capitalization, and punctuation.

# First, You . . .

Do you know how to blow a bubble? Do you know how to make a peanut butter and jelly sandwich?

Choose a task. Write the steps in the organizer. Use another sheet of paper if you have more than five steps. Then, look on the Internet to see how an "expert" explains how to do the task. Take notes. Write a paragraph telling how to do the task. Revise your steps to include some of the expert's steps. Use words such as *first, next, after,* and *finally* to connect your steps.

**Prewrite:** Use the organizer to plan your writing.

| How to _____ | |
|---|---|
| I say . . . | The expert says . . . |
| Step 1: | |
| Step 2: | |
| Step 3: | |
| Step 4: | |
| Step 5: | |

## ☀ Reflect and Revise

1. What makes someone an expert? Write a paragraph telling how a person can become an expert.

2. Edit your paragraph. Check for correct punctuation and spelling.

# What's for Dinner?

What's your favorite food for dinner? Perhaps you like tacos, lasagna, or hamburgers. Where does the food come from? If you said a restaurant or your mom, you have some research to do!

Choose a favorite food. Find out where the food comes from. Look on the Internet or in a cookbook. Some foods such as lasagna have several ingredients. Find out where all of the ingredients come from. Find out how the food is made. Then, write a paragraph explaining what you learned. Use words such as *first, next,* and *also* to connect your ideas. Include an illustration or photograph of the food.

**Prewrite:** Use the organizer to take notes.

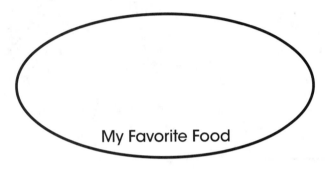

My Favorite Food

| What's in your food? | Where does your food come from? |
|---|---|
| | |
| | **How is your food made?** |
| | |

 **Reflect and Revise**

1. Who makes your favorite dinner food? Write a thank-you note to that person or company. Thank them for making your favorite food. Explain how you know the effort that goes into making the food.

2. Write a definition for at least three words in your paragraph. One word should have a suffix or prefix. Use a dictionary if needed.

# Good Question

How do airplanes fly? Why is the sky blue? How is a computer built? Who designed the first one-dollar bill? Inquiring minds want to know! What do you want to know?

Think of something you wonder about. Write your question in the organizer. Then, search the Internet or in books for an answer. Write a paragraph stating your question and explaining the answer you found. Include facts to support the answer.

**Prewrite:** Use the organizer to take notes.

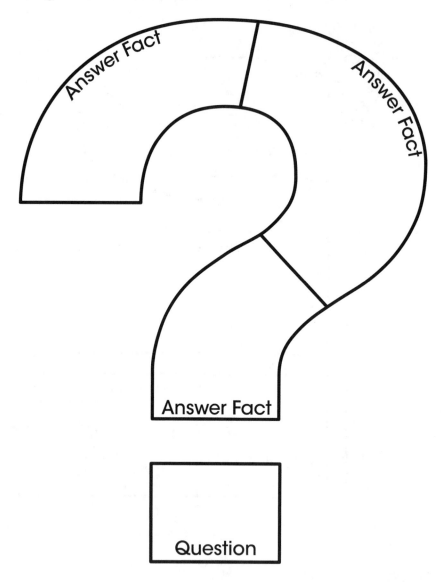

## Reflect and Revise

1. Do you think it is good to have questions? Why or why not?

2. Reread your paragraph. Revise your sentences to include at least one simple, one compound, and one complex sentence.

Name _____

# A Powerful Force

Force causes an object to move. How does force change motion? Try this experiment. Place one end of a book on a block to form a ramp. Roll a toy car down the ramp. Mark the spot where the car stopped. The ramp affected the amount of force needed to move the car. Now, add another block to make the ramp higher. What do you think will happen? Try it out.

Write the results on the organizer. Then, look on the Internet or in a book for more information about force and movement. Use the information you gather to write a science summary.

**Prewrite:** Use the organizer to write notes from your experiment.

| | |
|---|---|
| **Make a prediction.** What do you think will happen? | |
| **Test it and record.** What did happen? | |
| **Look for the answer.** What do the experts say? | |
| **Summarize.** What did you learn? | |

## ☀ Reflect and Revise

1. What else changes the amount of force needed to move an object? Plan another experiment. Try it out. Describe your experiment. Record your results.

2. Write the meaning of the word *force*. Then, write three words that have the word *force* as the base word. Use a dictionary if needed. Include the words in your paragraph if appropriate.

# Think Like a Scientist

Why do boats float and rocks sink? What makes stars twinkle? Why do the tides move in and out?

Look around you. What are questions you have about the universe or the way things work? Think of a science question you want to answer. Then, think like a scientist to find the answer. Use the Internet or books to find facts. Write a report about your findings. State your question. Then, explain the answer. Note the sources where you found the answer.

**Prewrite:** Use the organizer to think like a scientist.

| | |
|---|---|
| **Observe.** What do you see? | |
| **Ask a question.** What do you want to know? | |
| **Make a prediction.** What do you think the answer is? | |
| **Look for the answer.** Where can you find the answer? | |
| **Record the findings.** What did you find out? | |

## ☀ Reflect and Revise

1. Would you like to be a scientist? Explain why or why not.

2. Science reports are usually formal. Reread your report. Look at your word choices. Revise your writing to make it more formal.

## Endangered Animals

Dinosaurs are extinct. They no longer live on Earth. Sumatran elephants are endangered. Endangered animals are in danger of dying out. The forests where the elephants live are being cut down to make paper and palm oil. As the forested land is used up, many elephants die.

Look on the Internet for a list of endangered animals. Choose an animal. Use the Internet or books to find facts. Then, create a brochure to educate others. Use a brochure format on a computer. Or, fold a sheet of paper into thirds. Ask an adult to help you. Include facts about the animal. Tell why the animal is endangered. Then, create a cover with a title and a picture.

**Prewrite:** Use the organizer to group the facts.

| Facts about _____ | Where _____ Live | Endangered! |
|---|---|---|
| | | |
| | | What You Can Do |

## ☀ Reflect and Revise

1. Do you think it is important to help save endangered animals? Why or why not? Explain.

2. Check your brochure for correct spelling, capitalization, and punctuation.

# Giving Trees

*The Giving Tree* by Shel Silverstein (Harper & Row, 1964) is a classic story about a tree that gives its all for a boy. Trees do give a lot. Trees give shade. Trees give food. Trees give wood for shelter.

There are many different types of trees. Choose a kind of tree. Use the Internet to find three important facts about the tree. Write a two- or three-paragraph report about the tree. Include a picture.

**Prewrite:** Use the organizer to take notes.

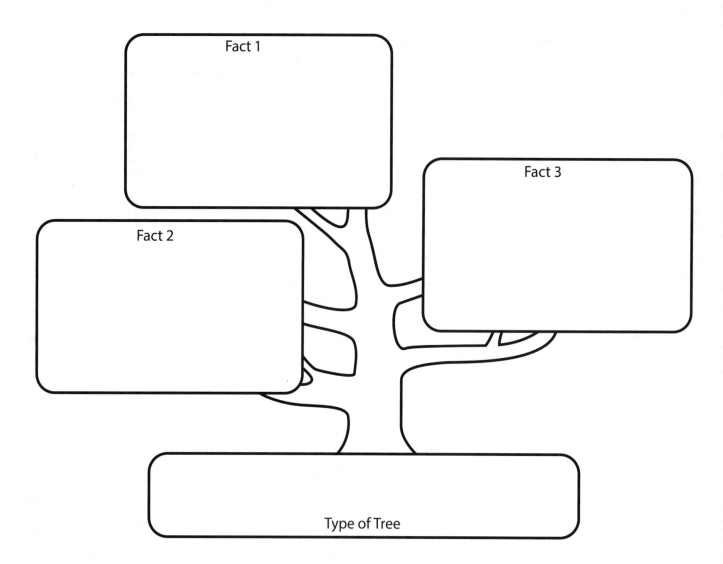

Fact 1

Fact 3

Fact 2

Type of Tree

## ⚡ Reflect and Revise

**1.** What do you like best about trees? Add a paragraph to your report explaining your opinion.

**2.** Check your report for correct spelling, capitalization, and punctuation.

# Nighttime Narrative

Do you like sleepovers? The family in this picture came up with a creative sleepover.

Study the picture. Look at the details. Think about what is happening in the picture. Talk to a friend about the picture. Then, write a story about the picture.

**Prewrite:** Use the organizer to plan your story. Remember: A good story has a problem and a solution. A good story has a beginning, middle, and ending.

| | |
|---|---|
| Title | |
| Characters | Problem |
| Setting | Solution |
| Beginning | |
| Middle | |
| Ending | |

## Reflect and Revise

1. Revise your story to include a dialogue between characters.

2. Read your story to a friend. Ask your friend if the dialogue between the characters seems believable. Revise your writing as needed.

# Getting to Know You

Think about one of your friends. Do you remember the first time you met your friend? What did you first think? How well do you know your friend? Part of becoming friends is getting to know each other.

Interview your friend. Think of four questions to ask your friend. Write questions that make your friend think. Write questions that help you know your friend better. Write questions that cannot be answered with *yes* or *no*. Then, write a report about your friend. Your report should include interesting details about your friend. End your report with a summary statement telling why you like your friend.

**Prewrite:** Write your questions on the organizer. Then, write your friend's answers.

| Questions | Answers |
|---|---|
| 1. | |
| | |
| 2. | |
| | |
| 3. | |
| | |
| 4. | |
| | |

## ☀ Reflect and Revise

1. Were you surprised by any of your friend's answers? Explain.

2. *Friendship* is an abstract noun. Abstract nouns name things you cannot see, hear, taste, touch, or smell. Write a definition of the word *friendship* using your friend as a concrete example.

## Motherly Advice

*Look both ways before crossing the street. Wash your hands before you eat. Do your best.* All mothers give advice. What is the best advice you have been given?

Write a narrative about a time your mother or a mother you know gave you some advice. Include a dialogue in your narrative. Be sure to have a beginning, middle, and ending.

**Prewrite:** Use the organizer to help you remember the conversation.

Mom _____

_____

_____ Me

_____

Mom _____

_____

_____ Me

_____

Mom _____

_____

_____ Me

_____

Mom _____

_____

_____ Me

_____

## ☀ Reflect and Revise

1. What is the worst advice you have been given? Who gave it to you? What happened? Write a story telling about the bad advice.

2. Edit your narrative. Check that you have used commas and quotations marks correctly in your dialogue. Revise as needed.

Name _____

# A Day in the Life of My Pet

Can you imagine life as a pet? Think about your pet or a pet that you know. What would it be like to live the pet's life?

Take some time to observe the pet. Then, research the pet on the Internet or in a book. Write a narrative about the pet. Include descriptive details. Be sure your writing has a beginning, middle, and ending.

**Prewrite:** Use the organizer to record your observations. Take notes as you read about the pet.

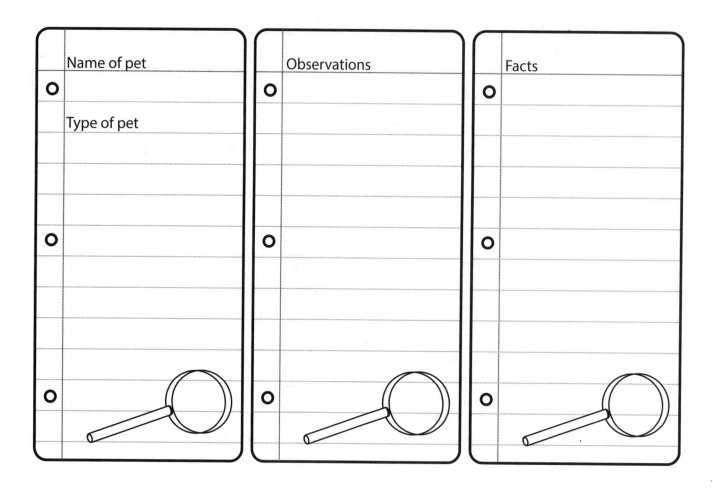

## ☀ Reflect and Revise

1. If your pet or a pet that you know could talk, what are three questions you would ask the pet? Write the questions. Then, write what you think the pet would answer.

2. Reread your narrative. Replace at least three words with synonyms that make your writing more descriptive. Use a thesaurus if needed.

Name _____

## When I Was One . . .

In the poem "Now We Are Six" by A. A. Milne, the author tells about a young child's yearly growth. Do you know what you were able to do at one year old? What about when you were two?

Read A. A. Milne's poem "Now We Are Six." The poem is available on the Internet. Talk to your family. Look at family pictures. Take notes on what new skill you were able to do each year. Then, write a personal narrative about you! Be sure to write about your growth in order. Add photographs.

**Prewrite:** Use the organizer to record your growth.

| | | |
|---|---|---|
| When I was 1... | When I was 2... | When I was 3... |
| When I was 4... | When I was 5... | When I was 6... |
| When I was 7... | When I was 8... | When I was 9... |

## ✺ Reflect and Revise

1. Write a poem about yourself using the same format as A. A. Milne's poem. Use information from your narrative.

2. Edit your narrative. Check for correct punctuation and spelling.

Name _____

# Remember When . . .

Everyone grows old. Sometimes older people lose their memories. Some people get Alzheimer's. Alzheimer's is a sickness. It makes it hard to remember. In the book *Wilfrid Gordon McDonald Partridge* by Mem Fox (Kane Miller Books, 1989), a young boy helps an old friend who is forgetful. He uses objects to help her remember. What memory could you share with an older person? How could you help the person remember?

Read the book to get some ideas. Use the Internet to find out more about memory loss. Then, write a narrative about a memory a person has forgotten. Think of an object you could use to help the person remember. Be sure your narrative has a beginning, middle, and ending.

**Prewrite:** Use the organizer to plan your writing.

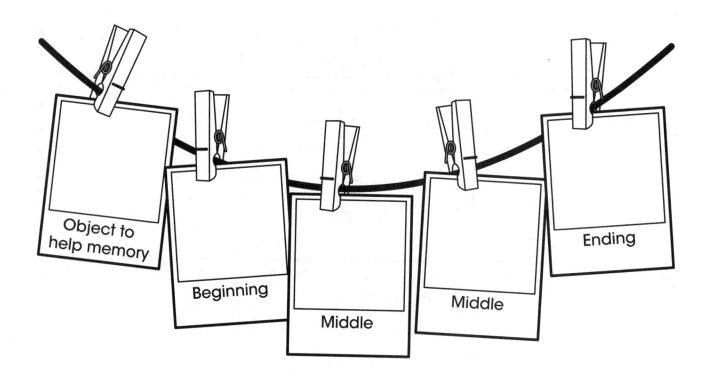

## Reflect and Revise

1. In what ways can you show kindness to an older person? Take time this week to be kind to an older person.

2. Reread your narrative. Use words such as *once*, *then*, *next*, and *finally* to connect the ideas. Signal words make writing easier to follow.

Name _____

## You Ought to Be in Pictures

What stories are told about you? Life stories are often repeated. Maybe you've heard stories about the day you were born. Or, maybe you've heard stories about your first day at a new school.

Interview family members, teachers, and friends. Look at photographs. Watch videos. Collect evidence about your life. Then, write a movie script starring you! Be sure your script has a beginning, middle, and ending.

**Prewrite:** Use the organizer to plan your writing.

My Life by _____

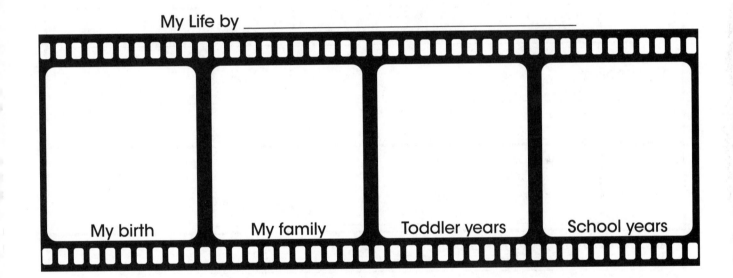

My birth     My family     Toddler years     School years

## Reflect and Revise

1. Think about your life up to now. What is one thing you would change about it if you could? Explain your answer.

2. Reread your movie script. Did you use a variety of sentence types? Revise your script to include simple, compound, and complex sentences.

# My Problem, My Solution

Have you ever lost a library book? Have you forgotten your homework at home? Have you missed your bus? These are all problems you might have had. Everyone has problems. Learning to deal with problems is an important life skill.

Use the Internet or books to find ways to solve problems. Write about a problem you had. Tell how you solved the problem. Then, write another way you could have solved the problem. Conclude your writing by telling the best way to solve your problem.

**Prewrite:** Use the organizer to plan your writing.

| Ways to Solve Problems |
| --- |
| • _____ |
| • _____ |
| • _____ |
| • _____ |
| My problem |
| How I solved my problem |
| Another way to solve my problem |
| Conclusion |

## Reflect and Revise

1. Tell about a time you had a problem that you didn't solve well. What happened? What should you have done differently?

2. Reread your writing. Did you use a variety of sentence types? Revise your writing to include simple, compound, and complex sentences.

Name _____

## And the Moral of the Story Is . . .

Have you read "The Tortoise and the Hare" or "The Grasshopper and the Ants"? These are fables. Fables are short tales with a lesson. Fables often use animals as characters.

Go to the library or look on the Internet to read some fables. Work with friends to brainstorm a list of lessons from the fables. Then, brainstorm a list of animal similes such as *sly like a fox* or *as wise as an owl*. Use the Internet to help you brainstorm. Write your own fable. Choose a lesson from your list. Use animal characters in your fable. Be sure your fable has a beginning, middle, and ending.

**Prewrite:** Use the organizer to plan your writing.

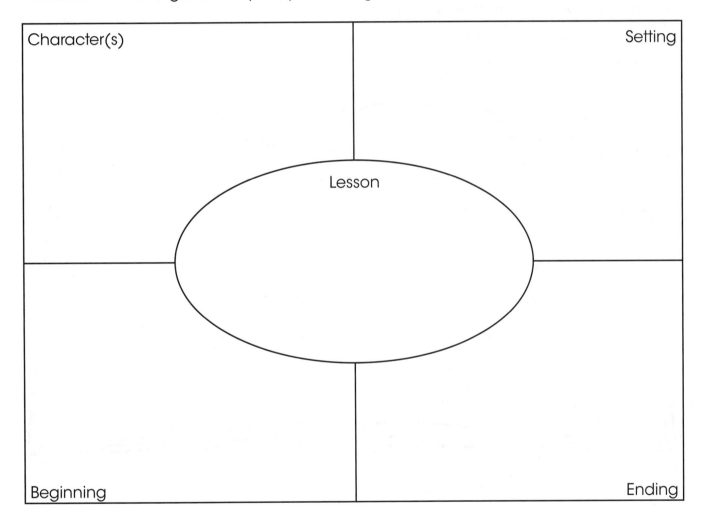

Character(s)

Setting

Lesson

Beginning

Ending

## ☀ Reflect and Revise

1. How would your fable be different if you changed the setting? Rewrite your fable with the setting in another time or place.

2. Did you use dialogue in your fable? If not, revise to include a dialogue. Check that you have used commas and quotation marks correctly.

Name _____

# Mixed-Up Fairy Tales

Once upon a time, they lived happily ever after. Fairy tales are magical. Many fairy tales begin with *Once upon a time*. They often end with *happily ever after*. The characters often live in castles. The setting can be *long ago and far away*.

Look in a book of fairy tales. Make a list of fairy tale titles. Complete the organizer. Then, write a new fairy tale. Mix up the characters and settings. Change the problems and solutions. For example, write a story about Snow White being locked in a high tower. Kissing a frog solves her problem. Be sure your fairy tale has a beginning, middle, and ending.

**Prewrite:** Use the organizer to list characters, settings, problems, and solutions. Circle the ones you will use to write your fairy tale.

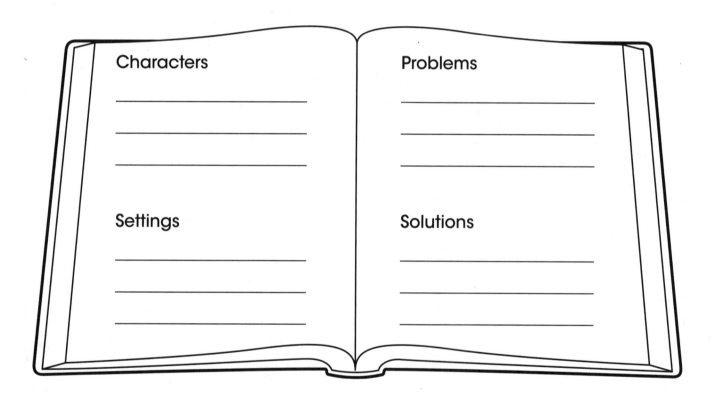

Characters

Problems

Settings

Solutions

## ☀ Reflect and Revise

1. Reread your fairy tale. How would your story change if the setting were in modern times? Revise your fairy tale with a setting in today's world.

2. Read your fairy tale to a friend. Ask your friend to retell the beginning, middle, and ending of your fairy tale. If these parts aren't clear, revise as needed. Use signal words such as *next, after,* and *before*.

# The Trail of Tears

Early in American history, the Cherokee American Indians were forced from their homes. They had to move from Georgia to Oklahoma. They had to walk many miles. Men, women, and children traveled this difficult path. Many suffered. Some died. This journey is called the Trail of Tears.

Use the Internet or books to find out more about the Trail of Tears. Then, write a story from the point of view of a person who traveled the trail. Use facts in your story. Add your own ideas about how the person might have felt.

**Prewrite:** Use the organizer to take notes. Then, use the notes to plan your story.

| Research notes |
| --- |
| Fact 1: |
| Fact 2: |
| Fact 3: |
| Fact 4: |
| Fact 5: |

| Story plan |
| --- |
| Characters: |
| Setting: |
| Beginning: |
| Middle: |
| Ending: |

## ☀ Reflect and Revise

1. Think about what you read about the Trail of Tears. Could the problem of land have been settled in a different way? Write a letter to President Jackson telling your ideas.

2. Edit your story. Underline each verb. Do the verbs agree with their subjects? Are the verbs the same tense throughout the story? Revise as needed.

# On the Move

From the beginning of time, people have been on the move. Early travelers walked. Later, people sailed on ships, rode on wagons, and traveled by train. Today's travelers drive cars, fly in planes, and take rockets into space.

Search the Internet and books to learn about a form of transportation. Then, write a story about travelers. Use the facts you learned to make your writing more interesting. Be sure your story has a beginning, middle, and ending.

**Prewrite:** Use the organizer to list the facts you learned. Then, plan your story.

| Form of transportation |  |
|---|---|
| Facts I learned <br><br> • <br><br> • <br><br> • |  |
| Characters | Setting |
| Problem | Solution |

## ☀ Reflect and Revise

1. How would your story be different if the characters used a different form of transportation?

2. Use two comparative or superlative adjectives or adverbs in your story. Show them to a friend. Tell your friend what the words are modifying.

# In the Land of Dinosaurs

Where did dinosaurs shop? Answer: At the Dino-store! The riddle may be funny, but it's not true. Dinosaurs didn't shop. There were no stores. What do you think life was like when the dinosaurs were alive?

Write a story that takes place in the time of dinosaurs. Look on the Internet or in books to collect facts about dinosaurs. Use the facts to make your story believable. Think about how the facts will help you write your story's setting, characters, problem, or solution.

**Prewrite:** Use the organizer to take notes.

| Setting | Characters |
|---|---|
| • | • |
| • | • |
| • | • |
| **Problem** | **Solution** |
| • | • |
| • | • |
| • | • |

## ☀ Reflect and Revise

1. Do you think adding facts to a fictional story makes the story more interesting? Why or why not?

2. Edit your story. Make sure you have used commas correctly. Revise the punctuation as needed.

Name _____

# Going for Gold

Gabby Douglas went from cartwheels to gold medals. In 2012, she won two Olympic gold medals in gymnastics. Athletes from around the world enter the Olympics. But, only a few win a gold medal.

Choose an athlete. Use the Internet and books to find out more about the athlete. Then, write a biography about the athlete. Include a picture of the athlete.

**Prewrite:** Use the organizer to take notes.

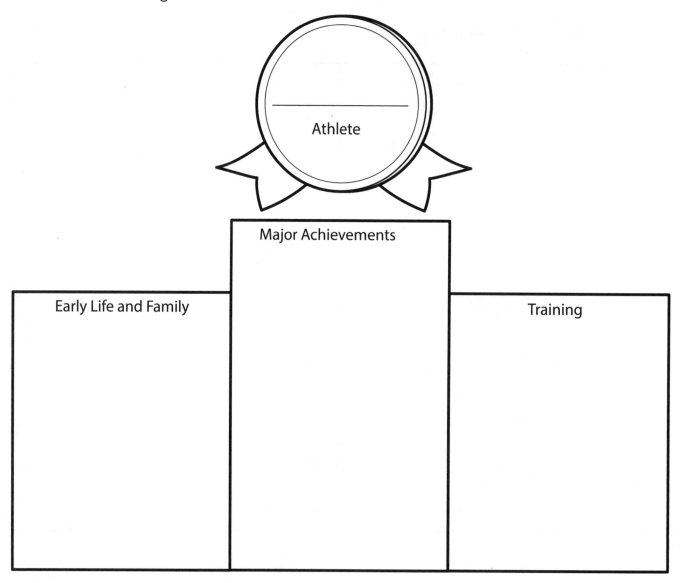

Athlete

Major Achievements

Early Life and Family

Training

## Reflect and Revise

1. Compare your life to the life of the athlete. How are your lives alike? How are they different? Draw a Venn diagram to show the comparison.

2. Does your biography include words to show time, such as *after*, *later*, or *finally*? If not, revise your writing to include time words.

Name _____

# Go Wild!

*Lions and tigers and bears. Oh my!* Animals in the wild are interesting to study. For example, the lion is known as the king of the jungle. But, lions like to sleep! They can sleep 16 to 20 hours a day.

Choose a wild animal. Look on the Internet or in a book. Find facts about the animal. Find at least three facts for each subtopic listed on the organizer. Then, write a report on a computer. Write a paragraph for each subtopic. Write an ending paragraph to summarize the key ideas. Include a picture.

**Prewrite:** Write the facts you find on the organizer.

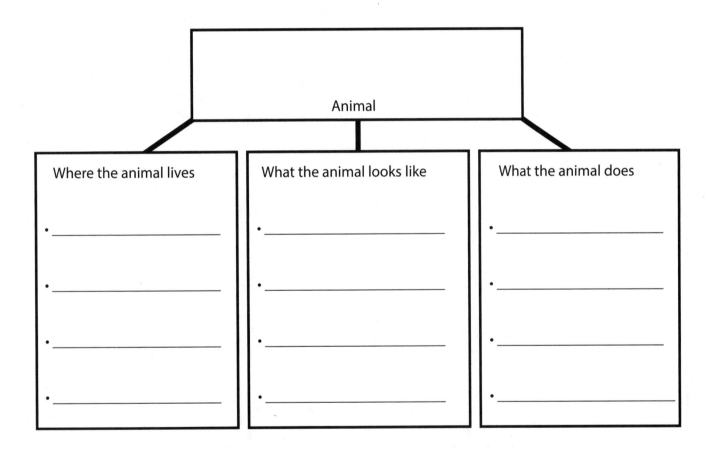

Animal

Where the animal lives

- _____
- _____
- _____
- _____

What the animal looks like

- _____
- _____
- _____
- _____

What the animal does

- _____
- _____
- _____
- _____

 **Reflect and Revise**

1. Do you think your animal would be happy in a zoo? Explain your answer.

2. Include a new vocabulary word in your report. Define the word using context clues.

# Body Works

You are sitting while you read this. But, your body is busy working. Your brain is thinking. Your heart is pumping blood. Your lungs are taking in oxygen.

Choose a part of the body you want to know more about. Look on the Internet and in books to learn about the body part. Then, write a report. Your report should have three paragraphs. Include a picture.

**Prewrite:** Use the organizer to take notes and plan your report.

| Body part | | |
| --- | --- | --- |
| What it looks like and where it is | What it does | How to care for it |
| • | • | • |
| • | • | • |
| • | • | • |
| • | • | • |

## ☀ Reflect and Revise

1. Every body part has an important function. Imagine your life without the body part in your report. Could you live? How would your life be different? Write about it.

2. Check your report for correct spelling. Use a dictionary if needed.

Name _____

# Desert Life

At first glance, the desert may look lifeless. But, further investigation will show it is filled with life. Many plants and animals make the desert their home. Each plant and animal has adapted ways to keep cool and use less water.

Choose one desert plant or animal. Use the Internet or books to find out how the plant or animal lives. Learn how it adapts to the harsh desert. Look at the organizer. Read the subtopics in the ovals. Find two facts for each subtopic. Then, write a report based on your research. Write each subtopic and its facts in a separate paragraph. Include a picture.

**Prewrite:** Use the organizer to take notes.

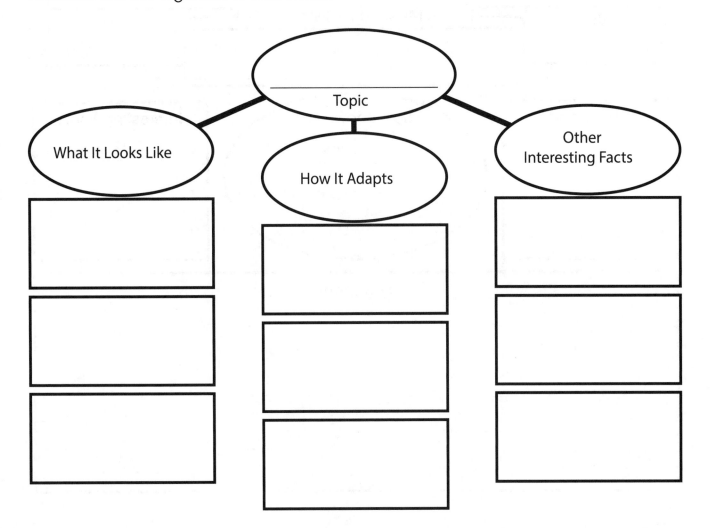

# Reflect and Revise

1. Would you like to live in the desert? Write a paragraph to explain your answer. Use the facts you learned. Add your paragraph to your report.

2. Check your report for correct spelling. Use a dictionary if needed.

Name _____

# Heroes in History

Martin Luther King Jr. marched for equal rights. Terry Fox ran to aid cancer research. Jonas Salk developed a vaccine for polio. Many people in history have worked to make life better. We call these people heroes. Who is your favorite hero in history?

Choose a person you admire. Do research about this person. Then, write a report about the person. In your summary, write about how the hero made life better for others.

**Prewrite:** Use the organizer to plan your report.

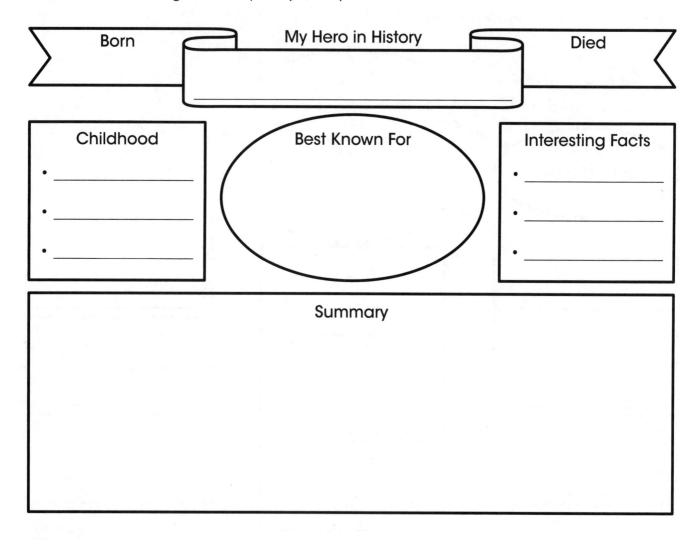

## Reflect and Revise

1. Think about a hero who is alive today. Compare today's hero to the hero in history. How are they alike? How are they different? Create a Venn diagram to compare the heroes. Add the comparison to your report.

2. Reread your report. Did you use a variety of interesting words? Substitute new words when appropriate. Use a thesaurus or dictionary if needed.

# Book News

*Extra, extra, read all about it!* Newspapers report the news. News reporters tell who, what, when, where, and why. These are the five Ws.

Use the five Ws to report on a favorite book. Use quotes from the book as evidence. Then, write your book report like a news story. Type your report on a computer.

**Prewrite:** Use the organizer to plan your report.

| | |
|---|---|
| Title:<br>Author:<br>Publisher: | |
| Who are the main characters?<br>*(Include names and descriptions.)* | Evidence from the book |
| What happened in the story?<br>*(Tell the main problem and the solution.)* | Evidence from the book |
| When did the story take place? | Evidence from the book |
| Where did the story take place? | Evidence from the book |
| Did you like the book? | Why or why not? |

## Reflect and Revise

1. What lesson did you learn from the main character of the book? Would you like to be like the character? Explain.

2. Look for words or phrases in the book that could have more than one meaning. Include at least one in your report.

Name _____

# Poor Pluto

Pluto was once the ninth planet. But, scientists now say Pluto is not a planet. It is a dwarf planet. A planet must orbit the sun. A planet must be a certain size. And, a planet must control the space around it. Sorry, Pluto! But, eight other objects in our solar system do fit these standards. There are a total of eight planets.

Choose one planet. Look for facts about the planet on the Internet or in books. Then, write a report about the planet. Consider making a model of the planet.

**Prewrite:** Use the organizer to take notes.

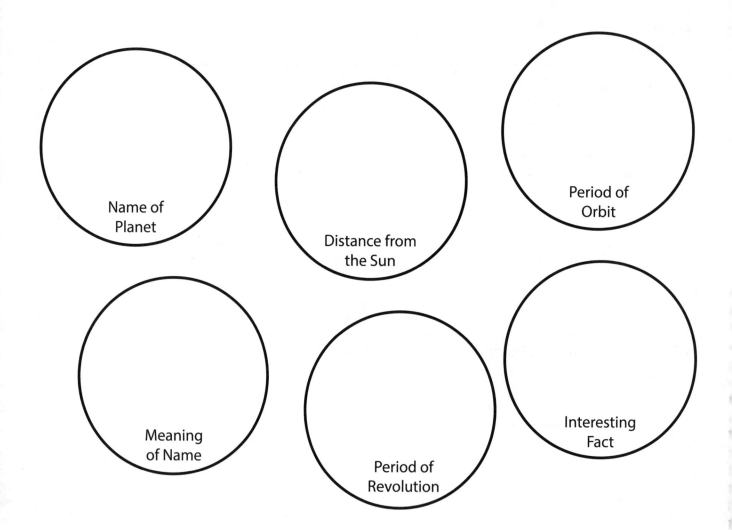

## ☀ Reflect and Revise

1. Write a science fiction story. Use your planet as the setting. Include facts in your story.

2. Reread your report. Are there a variety of sentence types? Revise it to include simple, compound, and complex sentences.

# Backyard Safari

What animals do you see outside your home? If you live in a rural area, you might see foxes or deer. If you live in the suburbs, you might see squirrels or birds. If you live in the city, you might see spiders or ants. Go on a backyard safari. Look for animals that make their homes outside your home. Write or draw what you observed on the organizer.

Then, choose one of the animals you observed. Use the Internet or books to learn about your natural neighbor. Use the information to write a report. Include a picture of the animal in the animal's home.

**Prewrite:** Use the organizer to take notes.

| My Observations | | |
| --- | --- | --- |
| | Animal | |
| What it looks like | Where it lives | Other interesting facts |
| | | |

## ☀ Reflect and Revise

1. Write a story from the point of view of the animal. Imagine how the animal feels to have you as a neighbor. Include the information you learned from your report.

2. Reread your report. Did you use correct capitalization and punctuation? Are all of the words spelled correctly? Use a dictionary if needed.

# The Big Blue Marble

Earth is sometimes called the big blue marble. From space, Earth looks blue. That is because most of Earth's surface is covered by water. Most of the water is in the oceans.

Choose one of the oceans to research. Look on the Internet or books to find information. Find facts about each subtopic in the organizer. Choose your own subtopic for the fourth paragraph. Then, write a report. Include pictures.

**Prewrite:** Use the organizer to take notes and plan your writing.

| Format | Facts to include | Notes |
|---|---|---|
| Paragraph 1: Introduction | • name of ocean<br>• location<br>• size | |
| Paragraph 2: Physical Characteristics | • ocean floor<br>• ocean layers<br>• temperature | |
| Paragraph 3: Ocean Life | • types of plants that live in the ocean<br>• types of animals that live in the ocean | |
| Paragraph 4: Conclusion | | |

## ⚡ Reflect and Revise

1. An oceanographer is a scientist who studies the ocean. Imagine you are a reporter. What questions would you ask an oceanographer for your report? List at least five questions. Then, look for the answers.

2. Check your report for correct spelling. Use a dictionary if needed.

# Be Prepared

The Boy Scouts have a motto: *Be prepared.* That's smart for staying safe during a natural disaster. Earthquakes, tornadoes, blizzards, and hurricanes are natural disasters. It is good to know the facts. Nothing can stop a natural disaster. But, knowing the facts and being prepared can help keep you safe. What disasters can happen where you live? Are you and your family prepared?

Use the Internet to learn more about a natural disaster. Learn facts about the disaster. Learn ways to stay safe. Then, write a report.

**Prewrite:** Use the organizer to take notes.

|  |  |
|---|---|
| Disaster | |
| Fact 1 | Fact 2 |
| Way to be prepared | Way to be prepared | Way to be prepared |

## ✴ Reflect and Revise

1.  Talk with your family. Write a plan for being prepared in a disaster. Review the plan at least once a year.

2.  Reread your report. Did you use any new vocabulary words? If so, define the words. If not, revise your writing to include at least two new words. Use a dictionary or thesaurus if needed.

# Answer Key

*Because writing is personal and presentations are unique, there are no "correct" answers" to be applied to students' work. However, students should follow the instruction of the writing prompts, fill in the graphic organizers, and apply the steps of the writing process. Use the guidelines below or the Common Core–Aligned Writing Rubric on page 4 to help you assess students' work.*

## Pages 6 to 10: Writing Practice Packet

Check students' work throughout the writing process practice pages. Help students master each step before going on to the next step. This process can be used with other writing prompts if more practice is needed before independent writing can begin. Refer students back to specific practice pages as needed.

## Pages 11 to 63: Reflect and Revise

The Reflect and Revise section at the end of each page asks students first to consider an alternative or additional slant to their topic. Often, they are requested to add this additional layer of thought to their writing. Check that they have fulfilled the challenge and that their conclusions have been applied to the writing if asked. Because the Common Core language standards are tied so tightly to the writing standards, the second part addresses specific language skills. Check through written work for mastery.

## Pages 11 to 24: Opinion/Argumentative Writing

Check graphic organizers. Writing will vary, but opinions should be supported with reasons and show evidence based on research, interviews, or recollection of experiences. Look for application of critical thinking and personal reflection.

## Pages 25 to 40: Informative/Explanatory Writing

Check graphic organizers. Writing will vary but should be based on research or interviews. Look for facts rather than opinions. Information should be presented using the structure of an introduction, body, and conclusion. Facts should be grouped in paragraphs according to subtopic. Ideas should be connected with linking words and phrases.

## Pages 41 to 53: Narrative Writing

Check graphic organizers. Stories and other narrative formats will vary but should respond to all of the items in the prompt. Look for clear and logical sequences of events using a variety of transitional words and phrases. Stories should include characters and setting as well as problems and solutions.

## Pages 54 to 63: Research Writing

Check graphic organizers. Reports will vary but should be based on research or interviews. Assess students' abilities to examine topics and convey ideas and information clearly to their readers. Students should use logical organizational structures, including introductory and concluding sentences or paragraphs.